The 22 Laws of Inner Peace

1862

by

Eliphas Levi

ISBN: 978-1-63923-209-3

Printed: May 2022

Cover Art By: Amit Paul

Published and Distributed By:
Lushena Books
607 Country Club Drive, Unit E
Bensenville, IL 60106
www.lushenabooksinc.com/books

ISBN: 978-1-63923-209-3

"The most precious asset of all is inner peace, and it must be preserved at all costs."

— *Fables & Symbols, 1862*

The
22 Laws of
Inner Peace

The
22 Laws of
Inner Peace

– 1862 –

by Eliphas Levi

The purpose of esoteric philosophy is to give us
that inherent serenity of soul which is the life of
heaven and the profound peace of the elect.

To achieve this peace it is necessary:

"The force which we call desire or will (two forms of the same force) draws together you and the thing you desire, and you are bound to go to the place where that thing can be found and that desire gratified."

— *Annie Besant, 1910*

"The object in magic is to overcome any force that opposes us."

— *The Dayspring of Youth, 1931*

EDITOR'S NOTE: This book is made up of excerpts that have been translated from French into English. Some of the excerpts appear in their entirety. The verbs 'will', 'wish', 'want' and 'desire' are often synonymous. The miniature posters at the end of the book are designed to improve your life by positively impressing your mind on a daily basis. Remembrance is key.

HOW TO USE THIS BOOK TO ILLUMINATE YOUR MIND:
1. Read it more than once each year. Repetition is necessary because we only absorb a small portion of what we read.
2. Place one of Levi's quotes where you will see it often. Reminders are essential to uproot unwanted habits.
3. Text message Levi's quotes to your friends and relatives. To learn, teach.

Contents

LAW 1

To believe in the wisdom of God and in the harmony of nature's laws. This faith will prevent us from prejudging evil and from getting annoyed at the appearances of a disorder that we don't have a remedy for, because what appears disordered to us is often the result of an order that escapes us. We will find in this thought the great secret of resignation.

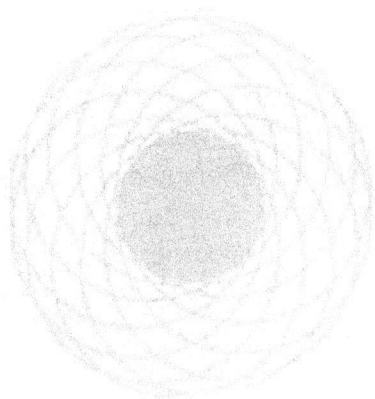

LAW 2

To never be disturbed by the apprehension of evil, because the evil that can reach us is never stronger than us. There is only one real evil, it is injustice and we can be just. The adversities foreign to our consciousness are the tests or the goodness of divinity. Let us await them with a smile.

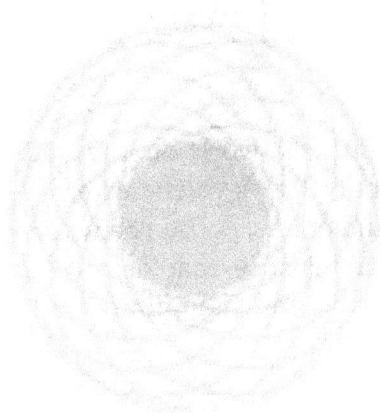

LAW 3

To continuously work on the reform of our character. By flaws of character one torments oneself and others. A bad character is therefore a habit of injustice that deserves and always brings trouble and disapproval.

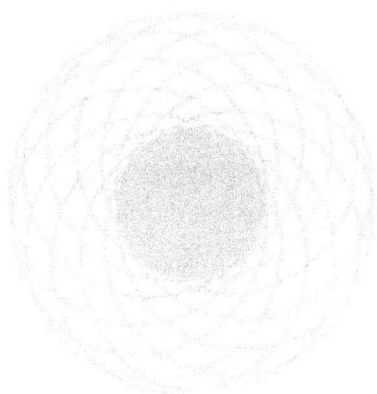

LAW 4

To never give oneself entirely to pleasure.
Pleasure is made for us, but we are not made for
it.

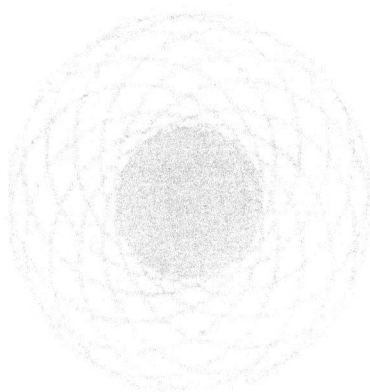

LAW 5

To seriously believe in the indestructibility of all that is good, all that is true, all that is beautiful, and all that is pure.

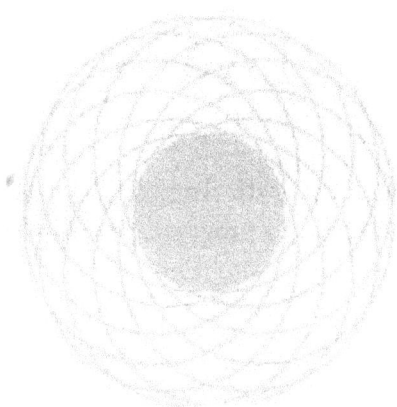

LAW 6

To believe that suffering is a work, work a struggle, struggle a progress, progress real life.

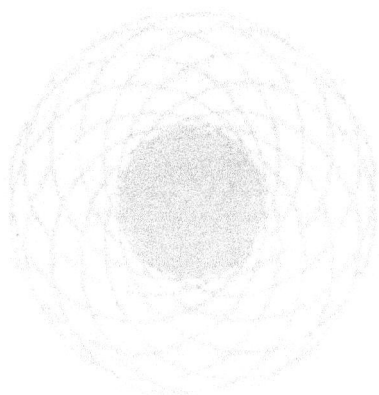

LAW 7

To not allow the cynicism of disbelief to occur before us.

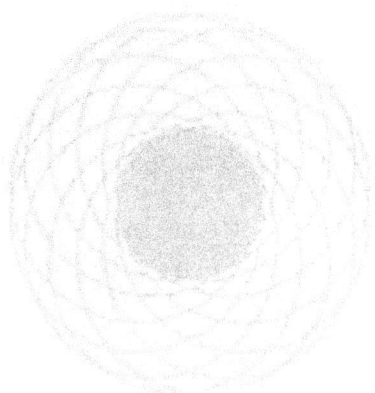

LAW 8

To believe in the reality of all that is good, even in life's most temporary forms. A glass of water that is given to us when we are thirsty deserves eternal life, said the great initiate, it is therefore of infinite worth, as are all things that come from God.

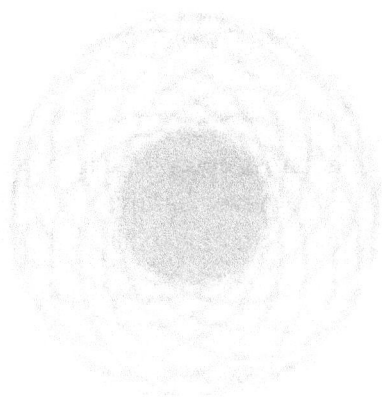

LAW 9

To never fear bankruptcy in the house of God, which means to never believe that there is no more spirituality in the world and that truth goes.

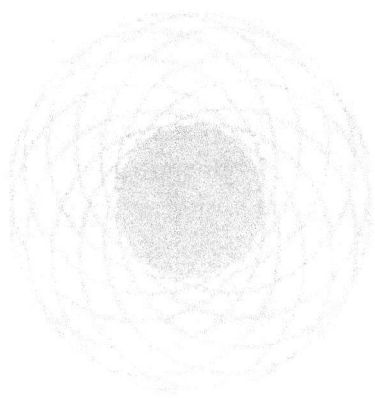

LAW 10

To be humble and to never believe that we are great because we have a great science or have great thoughts. A dewdrop reflects all the glories of a beautiful day, but none of them belong to it: it is the same with our soul. The sun drinks the dew and God can withdraw from us all of our intelligence and all of our genius. Like a drop of water, we are nothing but trembling and fleeting mirrors, and if nature breaks us, nothing empty will be made in the immensity. Heaven doesn't need us, it is us that needs heaven.

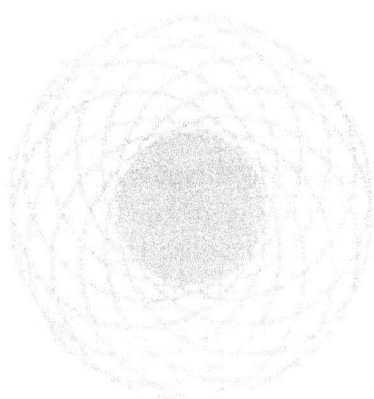

LAW 11

To protect oneself from the childish beliefs that disturb the conscience and above all to hold this idea in horror: that God wants to confuse human reason and be honored by the prejudice of madness, that like the sphinx he gives us riddles to guess and that he kills or forever tortures those who guess them and those who, not guessing them, don't worry about them. In actual fact God's supreme reason wants to elevate man's reason up to itself by faith in His correctness and justice, the God of the sages being the light of generous souls and not the gloomy agitation of the cowardly and groveling ones.

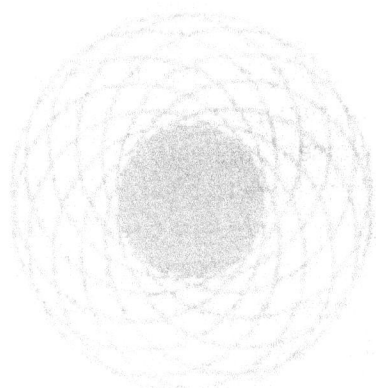

LAW 12

To raise the independence of one's consciousness above all human influences and all fears, because nothing worse than death can happen to us. In fact, we don't have to be afraid of death, as it is a natural and necessary thing from which the independence and greatness of the mind escape when the mind becomes firmly fixed on eternal truth and justice.

LAW 13

To never suffer from a love. To love because one should and because one wants to. Love becomes glorious when it is never shameful. The joys of love follow the one who never buys them with infamy. To prefer one's pleasure to one's honor is to be a coward. In fact, by cowardice one becomes unworthy of love, even the love of a tramp. A woman despises the man she degrades, and when she feels despicable, she respects the man who despises her.

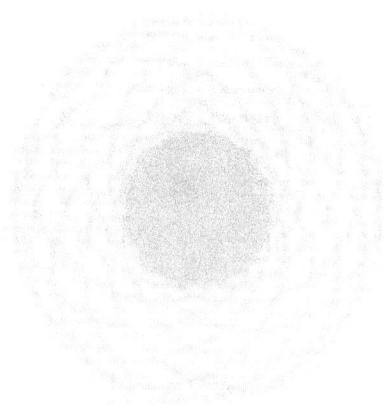

LAW 14

To not leave to divinity the effort of doing our work. To never complain about an evil that we can prevent. To dream that the fight against evil is our first duty and that we would be stupid and impious if we attributed to God the inconveniences that result from our own foolishness or laziness.

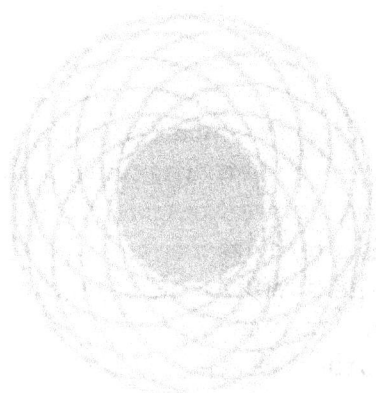

LAW 15

To not seek infinity outside mental and emotional balance. The whole world is not big enough to fill our soul, it is longing for an infinite perfection, and that is proof enough that it is immortal. The riches of the earth, when they are immense, become immense embarrassments and never satisfy their owner. The greatnesses of the world are often great despairs. Everything that can end is already as finished, and the vulture of Prometheus returns to enlarge the emptiness that is constantly in the heart of a man who is chained to the rock of power, because, the higher one places oneself above others, the lonelier one is, and God places an infinite weight on the isolation of pride.

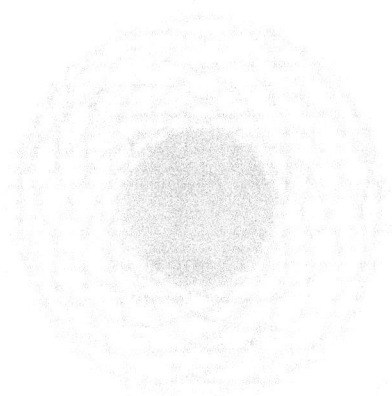

LAW 16

To not believe in illusions. As the realities of God are a thousand times more beautiful than the dreams of man, it is never necessary to content oneself with dreaming about what one can appreciate and know. Youth, friendship, love, poetry, glory, all of these are true, all of these are eternally true, though they all change areas like spring. Spring is not an illusion for the swallows; they have the courage to follow it and they always find it again.

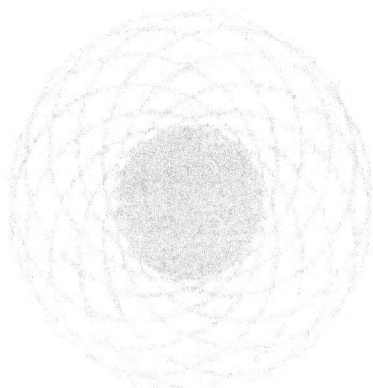

LAW 17

To do one's duty in the present and to never fear the future. To be happy when happiness presents itself as if we had only one day to live, as long as we find happiness in the satisfaction of an eternal need. The abandonment to God, the confident joy in the middle of nature's celebrations, the cheerfulness that soaks itself with light and sunshine, the enthusiasm for what is beautiful, the devotion to what is good, all of these don't calculate, don't reason with the worry of tomorrow. Horace said, "Happy is he who every night can say to himself: today I have lived, even if tomorrow a storm comes, it won't take away from me the serenity of the day that is ending." "Don't think about tomorrow," said Christ, "for tomorrow will have its own thinking to do. Each day has enough trouble itself."

Do you want to have nothing to fear for tomorrow? Do good today, good actions are the seed of happiness.

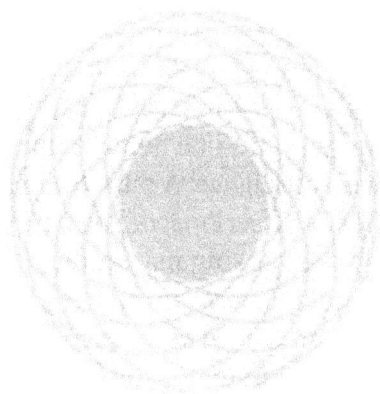

LAW 18

To obey the law, to go beyond one's duty, but never to put up with servitude. The death of the martyrs was sublime because one wanted to assault their conscience. A man doesn't renounce his beliefs, his affections, or his national habits because an overbearing master demands it. You can keep quiet before an oppression, you can refrain from an armed resistance, but then you pray and die by kissing the altar of the nation.

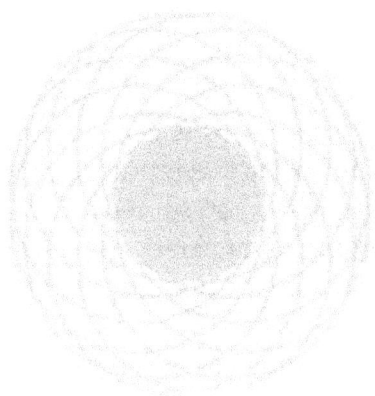

LAW 19

To never argue about God's essence. Faith in God must make men better and not misplace their reason. How can we define infinity? How can we explain what we don't understand? The more one reasons, the less one adores. Let us reason as much as we like about our need to adore, but when we pronounce the name of the indefinable, what supreme silence is kept among us! Let us prostrate and adore! It is not the elephant of the Brahmans, nor the three-headed elder of the Gnostics, nor is it anything blessed by the idolatry of nations. It is nothing that we can see, touch, hear, taste or articulate. It is what we must adore in the profound peace of the mind and in the enthusiasm of the heart.

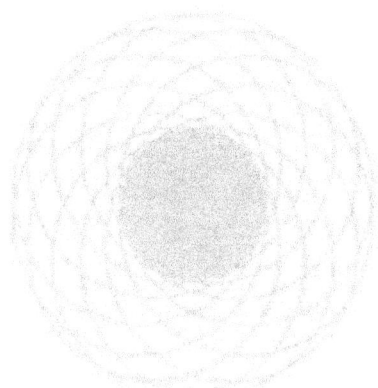

LAW 20

To respect the consciousness of others and to never impose even the truth upon them. To not break by force the yoke of the slaves who love their yoke. To always have devotion, but never too much zeal. The mad enjoy their madness, it would be too cruel to remove it from them without giving them reason in return. It is therefore necessary to have patience, it is necessary to let the fakir have his chain and the old world its idols until all of it falls by itself. Let us not waste our time giving useless speeches criticizing darkness; let us make the light shine, but not the light of a torch that sets fires. Let us no longer cover the statue of Jupiter nor the one of Saint Nicholas, a stupid population would adore Saint Nicholas regardless. Philosophers, respect the relics, if you don't want someone to burn your books. The light shines for everyone, but everyone has the right to open and close their eyes as they please.

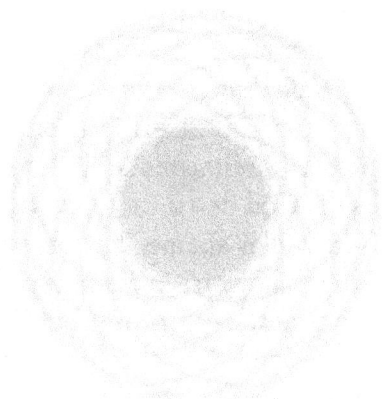

LAW 21

To not give evil a real existence. God, indeed, doesn't want it; nature rejects it, pain protests against it. Rational creatures cannot want it. Universal harmony doesn't have a place for it. Life constantly triumphs over it like death. Satan would therefore not know how to be king: he is the last slave of the fatality that he wanted. The eternal condemnation of evil is in the eternal triumph of good. Order remedies disorder by agony, and the agony itself is good, as it is a remedy. Besides, evil condemns and destroys itself by itself. God destines it to eternal agony. Pride is a crown of shame, lust an abortion of pleasure, greed the worship of misery. The paths of evil are wide at the beginning, but they shrink as one advances and they end in suffocation, by the prolonged crushing of their victim. They eventually become dead ends where one must perish if one doesn't have the courage and strength to turn back. Someone said, to prove the existence of another life, that bad people can be happy in this world. That is not true: the last and the most unhappy of men are the bad ones.

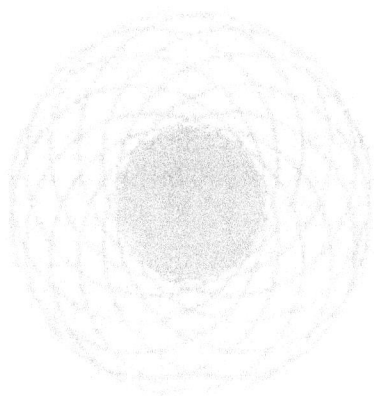

LAW 22

To not seek the glory that comes from the premature admiration of men, but the one that comes from honor, this consciousness of justice and devotion, which sooner or later will produce its splendor. Men end up subjecting themselves to the influence of genius and talent; but they hate those things, because the passion and the torment of the weak is envy. Glory for them is nothing but a triumph of selfishness, because they don't understand it otherwise, selfish that they are. They always deny devotion and go looking for some servile and infamous reason to sacrifice the heroes of humanity. Let them say what they want, as they want to speak without knowing and they don't want to listen. They gladly crown the uselessness that doesn't obscure them. Let us not need their crowns; one day they will have to bring them to our graves. And besides, if they got the grave wrong, what would happen to our corpses, what would especially happen to our souls, if, as we do not doubt, our souls survive the errors of the earth? Let us love good for the sake of good, science for the sake of science, beauty for the sake of beauty, truth for sake of truth. Do you think that Homer wrote his admirable poems for donations that he nevertheless needed? The cities of Greece rejected his misery, they argued about his birth and his name, and no one knows exactly which city gave him the supreme honors and deserved to have his remains.

"Let the dead bury their own," said Christ. "Seek first the kingdom of God and his Justice, and everything else will be given to you."

Fables

– 1862 –

FABLE I

THE MOUNTAINEER AND THE MAN OF THE VALLEY

At sunrise, an inhabitant in a foggy valley hung his head sadly and said, "The skies have turned away from us. Nature is obscured!"

"No," replied a mountaineer. "Right now the skies are lit up. All across the blue sky everything is shining and pure. The day is not obscured, it is just the earth steaming. Instead of staying at home and complaining about the darkness that covers a portion of the countryside, get moving, and come with me to see the sunrise on the mountaintop."

Haters and idlers, who always drag themselves around to only find depression, embarrassment, mud and dust; straighten up and lift your heads. This world, which your vanity always blames, is not the boring place you think it is. Climb the mountain and expand your soul; stop being small and the world will be big.

Fable II

The Pervert and The Old Sleaze

Beneath a vine-covered alcove a pervert was stealing a bunch of ripe red grapes. An old sleaze, heavy with depression, sat near him, saying: "Oh, my woman is unfaithful, she has two-timed me! My friend, there is no such thing as love."

"That's true," replied the pervert. "I wouldn't like to contradict you. Just let me finish picking the last of these divine grapes, let me taste them to the last mouthful, and then soon I will cry out that there is no such thing as grapes!"

The fox from La Fontaine's fable, who criticized the grapes he could not reach, would have rejected the sweetest fruits of late autumn if he had been as silly and arrogant as human beings can be.

୭ To deny what we do not have, or what we do not understand;

୭ to dispute the existence of what we have lost;

୭ to insult the good fortune which, because of our fickleness, has gotten tired of following us;

୭ to cowardly throw pebbles under the feet of someone who is better at walking than us;

୭ to assume the right to be rude in the name of frankness;

ॐ to make Heaven responsible for our mistakes and bitterness.

– all of this can only be described as one thing: nonsense!

Fable III

The Rat

A certain rat got so fat that he thought he was an elephant, and to such an extent that he even stopped being afraid of cats and dogs. At some point he suddenly decided to start working on making his nose grow into a trunk, as he had no trunk and obviously needed one to be an elephant. He stopped eating because he had no trunk with which to pick up his food, and whilst waiting for the trunk to arrive, he withered away and starved to death.

Many people make the mistake of always acting according to the strengths or gifts they do not have.

Imagination is meant to be controlled by the reins of reason, otherwise it stifles wisdom.

Lies and injustices limit our willpower, and very often our biggest faults are the false virtues we think we have.

Fable IV

The Wizard and The Princess

Long ago, a famous wizard fell in love with a princess. Lying on a soft sofa, the beautiful woman would cover herself everyday with wonderful jewels. Everything around her would blossom by the touch of her smile. If she wanted some golden chains, some griffins, some goblins, a ring, a treasure, she would just have to say the word.

The wizard was a giant who had smashed some towers with a single blow, but when his wings were touched by weak love, he would sigh like a baby.

Lying softly on an Aleppian carpet, the princess yawned and looked bored.

"Handsome man," she said to her jealous lover. "What do your treasures do for me! It's you I love. But don't you know how to be less terrifying?!

"Wizards are supposed to be able to turn into anything they wish; you wizards can turn invisible but you don't know how to love.

"I'd love to see you in the charming form of a bluebird or hummingbird, sleeping on your lover's bosom. Oh, how I would cherish you if you would change into a hummingbird to feed from a flower in my mouth!"

"Is that all it takes?" said the giant, charmed. And so he transformed himself from an ogre.

Shining like a sapphire, as light as a bee, he approached her for loving kisses.

Then the tender princess grabbed him, pierced him with a needle and hung him from her hair, telling him, "Be happy!"

As long as a woman admires an unknown force and fears seeing this force escape her, she is admirable of devotion and sacrifice; but once she feels like a queen, she wants more: she wants to be both goddess and priestess, and she sacrifices her lover for the two insatiable idols that she hides at the bottom of her heart: her coquetry and her vanity.

FABLE V

THE RIVER AND THE STREAM

Not far from the course of a river, a little breakaway stream wound hurriedly across the grass and the fern. The boastful stream, very pleased with itself, mocked the slow river, which calmly and without distractions let itself be pulled steadily down the slope by the weight of its waters.

The river said to the stream, "Believe me, I worry less and arrive before you. Business is not done well in a hurry. In travel, shortcuts are rarely necessary, and to go faster, all you need is to go straight."

Fable VI

The Man and The Silver God

A pagan, the story goes, had a god of silver. What's more, he was poor and he begged the god to help him.

One night, while he was asleep, he saw the silver idol say to him, "You have me, what more could you want?"

The pagan thought about it, had the god melted and saw his wallet grow.

To avoid a future of mean stinginess, what is needed? A bit of fire.

The gods forgive audacity and help those who help themselves. In other words, they like people who are bold, courageous and strong. What they give us is what we take from them.

Fable VII

The Hedgehog

"Don't criticize me," said a hedgehog. "This is my shape, whether it hurts you or not, and people should hold me and take me as God made me."

"Hold you where?" they tell him.

People's greatest troubles often come from the deceptions of their selfishness; they want to be admired in their weaknesses; they want to be loved in their faults. Everyone dreams about the devotion of others, but nobody wants to be devoted.

"Your elbow is in my way."

"You're bothering me; get back."

"I will move a lot further back; I'm leaving!"

"My friend has left me! What an ungrateful person!"

"If you wanted to keep your friend, why didn't you remove your elbow?"

"That would have been a nuisance to me, and anyone who wants to be a nuisance to me is not my friend."

That is exactly what your friend thought.

FABLE VIII

THE MOTHER-LAMB AND HER SON

A little lamb who did not want to do as he was told escaped from his mother's care and went off one fine morning to explore unknown lands. He dreamed of distant barns on flower-laden fields and natural springs of milk.

He left without ever thinking that it might destroy his mother, who spent many days calling out for him sadly and without success. She almost pined away, lying on the straw listening to the wind.

One day she jumped up joyfully and rushed

to the door. It was her son brought back to her. The poor thing had lost most of his wool. He was dirty and covered in bites and wounds. His mother cleaned him, cared for him and comforted him.

An old ram who lived nearby said, "My dear, you're crazy to make such a fuss of that rebel. He deserves more anger than pity."

"How could I be angry with my son when he has no one but me to make him forget his troubles? How could I get upset when all I am feeling is happiness? I don't know anymore whether he behaved badly, but I know that I have found him again."

The love of a parent is always ready to forgive; it is an extension of divine love. But forgiveness cannot be tolerance. God always forgives past evil, he never tolerates present evil.

Fable IX

The Birds in Their Nest

The birds were warm and happy in their nest, crouched beneath their mother's wings. But they were growing. Feathers started to cover them, their wings began to spread. Squashed up together, they kept pushing one another in the nest that was now too small.

The little birds were unhappy. "Is Heaven

tired of looking after us? Why squash us up so much? Is it to make us fight?"

"No," their mother said, "it is to make you use your wings."

Instead of imitating the poor fools who blaspheme and curse, let us resign ourselves to suffering; it is our wings developing.

FABLE X

THE SPARROW

A sparrow that was overfed and caressed too much became ragged and unkempt, and was on the verge of dying from sadness.

One day his cage opened and he escaped. Farewell to the well-stocked feeder, farewell to the well-furnished table, farewell to the long-loving kisses.

In the open air he cleaned and preened his feathers. No longer in a cage, the sky gave him back his zest for life.

He often had to endure hardship, but God gave him a new heart. He was a poor wild wretch who became once more a beautiful bird.

That is how good emerges from misfortune. A split forehead gave birth to Minerva, and those who are frustrated by a life of pleasure get a new lease on life in hardship.

Fable XI

The Lioness

One morning the lioness tried to change the balance of fate: "You're not allowed to be the sole provider," she used to say to the male, "the female must be free. She has claws and teeth; watch out anyone who wants to fight her! Look out the imprudent males who try to beat her down beneath them!"

As she was talking to herself in this way, the lion arrives and wants to act the master. So the lioness says, "Thank God, the time has come to make myself known!"

She leaps onto her husband's neck, and despite his mane and tough skin, begins to strangle him like a professional. The lion, an old fighter, hardened to bloodshed, is taken by surprise by the villainess, so with great regret he hits out with his paw. A lion's paw, even when his claws are not out, carries a certain weight which always makes an impression. The lioness crawls away whining to show her neighbours her bloody wound:

"Look at the coward, the murderer! A weak female! An abused lover! Tearing her breast without respect, without modesty! By you or by the gods I must see him punished!"

So the neighbours gather together and the lion is judged and condemned. But the lioness also took care not to say that she had tried to strangle him.

Between husband and wife, neighbours, don't point the finger. Abuse of power is embarrassing, but was the weak person who cried in the right?

The worst of all tyrannies is that of the weak. Actually, there is hardly any other sort of tyranny than this one, as the strong do not oppress, they govern. The weak, on the other hand, do not govern, and how could they do so, when they do not control themselves.

Often power fails before the seductions of weakness. Then Delilah despises Samson and tells lies about him; she has to do this so that her betrayal is not embarrassing...Pale but smiling, she says, "Today I am his avenging angel and payback is mine! I was jealous!...He had too much love!"

FABLE XII

ODYSSEUS AND THE SEA

The sea was becoming smooth, murmuring and peaceful; the clouds of evening, torn apart by the wind, hung in the west, their golden tops showing the last splendours of the invisible sun. The coat of Thetis, striped red and gold, offered great depth to the great sky. Silence came over the earth and over the water, and a low sound seemed still to come from the sleeping seashore. Alone and without clothes, covered in salt from the sea, battered, but stronger than the hatred of the god, Odysseus stood on some dreadful rocks, and the evening stars showed him to Poseidon, saying : "The gods admire a hero when he comes through bad times to create good luck!"

Homer's symbolic poems are the great saga of the human spirit, its struggles and its initiation by victory over the elements. The Iliad is a our youth. It is about untamed passions; rival beliefs; gods who destroy each other.

There is Agamemnon, pride; Achilles, anger, and Thersites, envy, on the Greek side; and on the Trojan side Helen, lust, and Paris, cowardice or laziness. In this conflict of the forces of fate Troy falls, but its conquerors will soon perish. Only Odysseus, that is prudence combined with persistent courage, will triumph over all passions and all storms.

The Odyssey is our maturity; it is the initiation of the man who creates himself through an uninterrupted series of sacrifices and efforts. Odysseus triumphs over the Cyclopes, over Calypso and over Circe, but one by one he loses his companions, his riches, his ships and even his clothes, arriving on the island of the Phaeacians naked and alone.

The Phaeacians represent sages. Odysseus the king arrives among them stripped of everything, like a newborn infant entering into life. It is by his own merit alone that he will make himself known and that he will be able to win and keep his place at the table of king Alcinous. Odysseus is never greater than at the moment when, having lost everything, he comes out of the sea full of courage and self-confidence, further away than ever from losing the hope of once more seeing his country and sitting on Laertes' throne. What does he lack, in fact, to succeed? He knows, he desires, he dares and he keeps silent.

He no longer has anything; it is time to do everything; he carries with him his gods, his country and his fortune. He is more constant than fate, greater than misfortune, stronger than the storm and with a greatness wider than the sea.

What could he fear? He carries Providence within him and luck will obey him.

Fable XIII

The Horse and The Dog

One day a young scrawny horse was sent away to be slaughtered. Fortunately a farmer with high expectations intervened and bought him for almost nothing. The horse was then fed lots of grass and gradually returned to health.

Then the farmer loaded him up and overworked him so hard that one of his friends, an old dog, said, "Escape, get away. I'll gnaw through your bridle."

"No," replied the brave horse. "My master rescued me and raised me. How can I escape without those memories holding me back? I remember the good, I do, but as for the bad, is it worth remembering?"

What evil on earth is big enough to deserve a memory in the presence of goodness, and what fading mistake can ever leave a shadow on the splendid truth?

How to attract your desires, naturally and magically

– 1854 –

Magical operations are the exercise of a natural power, but superior to the ordinary forces of nature. They are the result of a science and a habit that raise the human will above its habitual limits.

The supernatural is only the extraordinary natural or the exalted natural: a miracle is a phenomenon which shocks the crowd because it is unexpected; the marvelous is that which marvels, it is made up of effects that surprise those who are ignorant of the causes or who assign them causes that are not proportional to the results. Miracles are only for the ignorant; but, as an absolute science barely exists among men, the miracle can still exist, and it exists for the whole world.

Let us start by saying that we believe in all miracles, because we are convinced and certain, even from our own experience, of their entire possibility.

There are some that we do not explain, but that we do not regard as less explicable. From the greater to the lesser and from the lesser to the greater the consequences are identically relative and the proportions progressively rigorous.

But, in order to perform miracles, it is necessary to be outside the common conditions of humanity; it is necessary to be either detached by wisdom, or exalted by madness, above all passions or outside them through ecstasy or frenzy. That is the first and most indispensable of the operator's preparations.

So, by a divine or predestined law, the magician can only exercise omnipotence in inverse proportion to his material interest; the alchemist makes even more gold the more he resigns himself to deprivations and the more he values poverty, the protector of the super-work's secrets.

The adept whose heart is without passion will dispose for himself of the love and the hatred of those who he will want to make instruments of his science: the myth of Genesis is eternally true, and God only lets the tree of science be approached by the men who are sufficiently abstinent and strong not to desire its fruits.

You therefore who seek in magic a way to satisfy your passions, stop yourselves on this deadly path: you would only find madness or death. It was expressed in the past by a vulgar tradition in which the devil would sooner or later end up strangling the sorcerers.

The magician must therefore be detached, sober and chaste, disinterested, impenetrable and inaccessible to every type of prejudice or terror. He must be without bodily defects and immune from all contradictions and all difficulties. The first and most important of magical works is to achieve this rare superiority.

We have said that passionate ecstasy can produce the same results as absolute superiority, and this is true as to the success, but not as to the direction of magical operations.

Passion strongly projects vital light and prints unforeseen movements on the universal agent; but it cannot retain as easy as it throws, and so its destiny resembles Hippolytus dragged by his own horses, or Phalaris suffering from the instrument of torture he had invented for others.

The human will fulfilled by action is like a cannonball that never recoils before an obstacle. When launched violently, it goes through it, or it enters it and loses itself within it; however, if it goes on with patience and perseverance, it is never lost, it is like the wave that always returns and ends up wearing away the iron.

Man can be modified by habit, which becomes, according to the proverb, a second nature in him. Through persevering and graduated gymnastics, the strengths and the agility of the body develop or create themselves in astonishing proportion. It is the same with the powers of the soul. Do you want to reign over yourselves and others? Learn how to will.

How can one learn to will? Here is the first secret of magical initiation, and the former depositaries of sacerdotal art surrounded the entrance of the sanctuary with so much terror and prestige in order to make the very essence of this secret understood. They only believed in a will when it had proven itself, and they were right. Power can only assert itself through victories.

Laziness and forgetfulness are the enemies of the will, and that is why all religions have multiplied their practices and made their teaching meticulous and difficult. The more one is annoyed by an idea, the more strength one gains in the sense of this idea. Don't mothers prefer those of their children who caused them the most grief and cost them the greatest care? Therefore the strength of religions exists entirely in the inflexible will of those who practice. As long as there is a worshipper believing in the holy sacrifice of the mass, there will be a priest to recite it to him; and as long as there is a priest reciting his breviary everyday, there will be a pope in the world.

The most outwardly insignificant practices,

outwardly foreign in themselves to the intended goal, still lead to this goal by educating and exercising the will. If a peasant woke up every morning at two or three o'clock and traveled very far from home everyday to pick a sprig of the same herb before sunrise he would be able to, while carrying this herb on him, perform a large number of prodigies. This herb would be a sign of his will and would become through this very will everything that he would want it to become in the interest of his desires.

To be able it is necessary to believe that one can, and this faith must be immediately translated into actions. When a child says, 'I can't', his mother replies, 'Try'. Faith does not even try; it begins with the certainty of finishing, and it works calmly as if it had omnipotence at its command and eternity before it.

You therefore who present yourselves before the science of the magicians, what do you want from it? Dare to formulate your desire, whatever it is, then get to work immediately, and do not stop acting in the same sense and to the same end: what you want will be done, and it has already begun for you and by you.

Sixtus V, while watching his cattle, had said: I want to be pope.

You are a beggar and you want to make gold: get to work and do not stop. I promise you in the name of science all the treasures of Flamel and

Raymund Lully.

"What needs to be done first?" You need to believe that you can, then act. "Act how?" Wake up everyday at the same time and early; wash yourself at a spring in all seasons before daylight; never wear dirty clothes, and for this clean them yourself if necessary; exercise voluntary deprivations, in order to better endure the involuntary ones; then silence every desire that does not belong to the accomplishment of the super-work. "What! By washing myself everyday at a spring I will make gold?" You will work in order to make it. "It is a mockery." No, it is a secret. "How can I use a secret that I don't understand?" Believe and do, then you will understand.

One day someone said to me, "I would like to be a devout Catholic, but I am a Voltairean. What wouldn't I give to have faith!" "Well!" I replied, "Don't say 'I would like' anymore; say 'I will', and do works of faith; I assure you that you will believe. You are a Voltairean, you say, and among the different ways to understand faith, the one you oppose the most is the one of the Jesuits and however to you it seems the strongest and most desirable...Do the exercises of Saint Ignatius, and repeat them without letting yourself get discouraged, and you will become a believer like a Jesuit. The result is infallible, and, if you then have the naivete to believe that it is a miracle, you are already mistaken in thinking that you are Voltairean."

A lazy person will never be a magician. Magic is an exercise of all hours and of all moments. It is necessary that the operator of great works be absolute master of himself; that he knows how to overcome the attraction of pleasure, appetite and sleep; that he is unresponsive to success as he is to insults. His life must be one will directed by one thought and served by entire nature, which he will have subjected to the spirit in his own organs, and by the sympathy in all the universal forces that are their correspondents.

All faculties and all senses must take part in the work, and nothing in the priest of Hermes has the right to remain idle; it is necessary for the intelligence to be formulated in signs and summarized in characters or pentacles; it is necessary for the will to be determined in words and for the words to be accomplished by acts; it is necessary to translate the magical idea into light for the eyes, harmony for the ears, smells for the nose, flavors for the tongue and forms for the touch; it is necessary, in a word, that the operator accomplishes in his whole life that which he wants to accomplish in the world outside him; he needs to become a *magnet* to attract the desired thing; and, when he is magnetic enough, he needs to know that the thing will come by itself and without him thinking about it.

How man & woman connect

– 1865 –

God and nature, authority and freedom, faith and reason, spirituality and science, are eternal principles that we have not been able to connect yet, but they exist, and as they cannot destroy one another, they should really work together.

The way to connect them is to make a clear distinction between them and to balance one with the other. Darkness is needed for light. It is the nights that define and measure the days. A woman should not try to become a man and a man should never take over a woman's empire, but both should unite to complete each other. The more a woman remains feminine, the more she deserves the love of the man; the more masculine a man is, the more trust he inspires in a woman.

Reason is the man; faith is the woman.

The man should let the woman have her mysteries, the woman should let the man have that independence which he likes to sacrifice for her. The father should never dispute the rights of the mother in her maternal domain; though the mother should never try to remove the paternal sovereignty of the man. The more they respect each other, the closer they will unite. There is the solution to the problem.

How to attract the positive

– 1869 –

It is said and repeated everyday that good people are unlucky in this world while the bad people prosper and are happy. This is a stupid and abominable lie.

This lie comes from the common mistake that confuses wealth with happiness; as if we could rightly say that Tiberius, Caligula, Nero and Vitellius were happy; they were rich though, and what's more they were masters of the world and yet their hearts had no rest, their nights were sleepless and their conscience was lashed by furies.

Does a pig become a man when we serve it truffles in a golden trough?

Happiness is inside us; it is not in our bowls, and Malfilâtre dying of hunger would have deserved his fate if he had wished he were a fattened pig.

Who is the happiest out of Socrates and Trimalcion (that character in Petronius who is Claudius' caricature)? Trimalcion would have died of indigestion if he had not been poisoned.

There are good people who suffer poverty and even depression, I do not deny this, but often it is their own fault and often however it is their very poverty which preserves their integrity. Wealth might corrupt and misplace them. We must not think that the truly good people are those who belong to the masses of fools, those with meagre courage and weak wills, those who obey laws out of fear or weakness, the devotees who fear the devil and the poor devils who fear God. All of these people are dumb cattle who do not know how to profit from gold, wealth or depression; but can one ever seriously pity the wise, the truly wise, whose occasional ill-treatment is always done by envy? But at this point many of my readers will say, with an air of disappointment, 'You promised us magic and have given us morals. We've had enough philosophy, tell us now about esoteric forces.' Okay, those of you who have read my books will know the meaning of the two snakes entwined around the winged staff. They are the two opposing currents of universal magnetism. The snake of creative and preserving light and the snake of eternal fire that devours in order to regenerate.

The good are magnetized, vivified and preserved by the imperishable light, the bad are burnt by the eternal fire.

There is a magnetic and sympathetic

communion between children and light; they all bathe in the same source of life; they are all happy about the happiness of one another.

Positive magnetism is a force that gathers and negative magnetism is a force that scatters.

Light attracts life and fire carries destruction with it.

White magnetism is compassion and black magnetism is aversion.

Good people love one another and bad people hate one another because they know everything about each other.

The magnetism of those who are good attracts to them all that is good and when it does not attract wealth it is because wealth would be bad for them.

How to read the sky

– 1854 –

A long contemplation of the sky exalts the imagination; the stars then respond to our thoughts. The lines drawn mentally from one star to the other by the first observers must have given men the first ideas of geometry. Depending on whether our soul is agitated or calm, the stars appear to be shining with threat or twinkling with hope. In this way the sky is the mirror of the human soul, and when we believe we are reading in the stars, it is in ourselves we read...

The wise man who wants to read the sky should also observe the days of the moon, whose influence is very strong in astrology. The moon successively attracts and repels the magnetic fluid of the earth, and that is how it produces the ebb and flow of the sea; he should therefore be well acquainted with its phases and know how to distinguish its days and hours. The new moon is favorable at the beginning of all magical works; from the first quarter to the full moon, its influence is warm; from the full moon to the third quarter, it is dry; and from the third quarter to the last, it is cold.

Here are the special characters of all the days

of the moon, marked by the twenty-two keys of the Tarot and by the signs of the seven planets:

1. THE MAGICIAN

The first day of the moon is that of the creation of the moon itself. This day is consecrated to mental enterprises, and should be favorable for opportune innovations.

2. ESOTERIC SCIENCE

The second day, whose genius is Enediel, was the fifth day of creation, for the moon was made on the fourth day. Birds and fishes, which were created on this day, are the living hieroglyphs of magical analogies and of the universal doctrine of Hermes. The water and the air, which were thereby filled its the forms of the Word, are the elementary figures of Mercury of the Sages, that is, of intelligence and speech. This day is conducive to revelations, initiations, and great discoveries of science.

3. THE CELESTIAL MOTHER

The third day was that of man's creation. So is the moon called the MOTHER in Kabbalah when it is represented in association with the number 3. This day is favorable to generation, and generally to all productions, whether of body or mind.

4. THE EMPEROR·

The fourth day is dreadful; it was that of the birth of Cain; but it is favorable to unjust and tyrannical enterprises.

5. THE HIEROPHANT

The fifth day is fortunate; it was that of the birth of Abel.

6. THE LOVER

The sixth is a day of pride; it was that of the birth of Lamech, who said to his wives, "I have slain a man to my wounding, and a young man to my hurt. If Cain shall be avenged sevenfold, truly Lamech seventy and sevenfold." This day is propitious for conspiracies and rebellions.

7. THE CHARIOT

On the seventh day, birth of Hebron, who gave his name to the first of the seven sacred cities of Israel. A day of religion, prayers, and success.

8. JUSTICE

Murder of Abel. Day of expiation.

9. THE HERMIT

Birth of Methuselah. Day of blessing for

children.

10. Ezekiel's Wheel of Fortune

Birth of Nabuchodonosor. Reign of the Beast. Fatal day.

11. Strength

Birth of Noah. Visions on this day are deceitful, but it is one of health and long life for children born on it.

12. The Victim

Birth of Samuel. Prophetic and cabalistic day, favorable to the fulfilment of the great work.

13. Death

Birthday of Canaan, the accursed son of Cham. Baleful day and fatal number.

14. The Angel of Temperance

Blessing of Noah on the fourteenth day of the moon. This day is governed by the angel Cassiel of the hierarchy of Uriel.

15. Typhon

Birth of Ishmael. Day of reprobation and exile.

16. The Blasted Tower

Birthday of Jacob and Esau; the day also of Jacob's predestination, to Esau's ruin.

17. The Twinkling Star

Fire from heaven burns Sodom and Gomorrah. Day of salvation for the good, and ruin for the wicked; on a Saturday dangerous. It is under the dominion of the scorpion.

18. The Moon

Birth of Isaac. Wife's triumph. Day of conjugal affection and good hope.

19. The Sun

Birth of Pharaoh. A beneficent or fatal day for the greatnesses of the world, according to the different merits of the great.

20. The Judgment

Birth of Jonas, the instrument of God's judgment. Propitious for divine revelations.

21. The World

Birth of Saul, material royalty. Danger to mind and reason.

22. INFLUENCE OF SATURN

Birth of Job. Day of trial and suffering.

23. INFLUENCE OF VENUS

Birth of Benjamin. Day of preference and tenderness.

24. INFLUENCE OF JUPITER

Birth of Japhet.

25. INFLUENCE OF MERCURY

Tenth plague of Egypt.

26. INFLUENCE OF MARS

Deliverance of the Israelites, and passage of the Red Sea.

27. INFLUENCE OF DIANA

Splendid victory achieved by Judas Maccabeus.

28. INFLUENCE OF THE SUN

Samson carries away the gates of Gaza. Day of strength and deliverance.

29. THE FOOL OF THE TAROT

Day of failure and miscarriage in all things...

To conclude this chapter we will state that magnetic intuitions in themselves interpret the worth and reality of all these cabalistic and astrological calculations, that are perhaps childish and totally subjective if done without inspiration, with cold curiosity and without a powerful will.

EDITOR'S NOTE: With regard to the effective use of a lunar calendar, take note of your social interactions and check to see if they are as positive or as negative as on the same lunar days of the next month. In other words, keep a diary and look for patterns. Rather than taking the author's calculations literally, use them as prods to investigation. For a free lunar calendar, lunarium.co.uk is recommendable.

The
Illuminating
Quotations
of Eliphas Levi

1810-1875

What one wants with perseverance, one does.

In the game of chess, to anticipate is to win, it is the same in the game of life.

Weak people talk and do not act, strong people act and keep silent.

You do not have to resign yourself to your chains if you can break them.

Calmness is the secret of strength.

Fear is nothing but a laziness of will.

Power is not given to us, one must take it.

The one who knows has no reason to doubt; when the mind does not doubt, the will does not hesitate, and then you get what you want.

To doubt is to go crazy; to stop is to fall; to step back is to jump into a hole.

All miracles are promised to faith; but what is faith if not the audacity of a will that does not hesitate in the darkness, and that walks towards the light through all hardships and overcoming all obstacles!

Have faith in love inseparable from logic. With this faith, if you know, if you desire, if you dare and if you have the art of keeping silent you will be stronger than the world and your wishes will be fulfilled by heaven and earth.

Everything is possible for the one who desires only what is true!

It is by absolute devotion that faith is proven and built.

What do obstacles matter to us? A brave one should not count his enemies before the battle. To anticipate evil is to make it somehow necessary. What will come to us is the result of what we desired: that is the universal prophecy.

The acts most indifferent in appearance, directed by an intention and repeated with persistence, make this intention succeed.

Put a huge passion at the service of a strong reason while hiding the reason and decorating the passion, there's the secret of success and of getting people carried away.

A great action always prepares an equal reaction, and the secret of great successes is entirely in the foreknowledge of reactions.

It is rivalry that often brings success: one always leans on what resists.

With the weak beings of today one must impress to succeed.

Boldness united with intelligence is the mother of all successes in this world. To begin, one must know; to accomplish, one must will; to will truly, one must dare; and to peacefully gather the fruits of one's daringness, one must keep silent.

Success is ability; constant misfortune is trying forever: these two quotes summarize the two opposing destinies of the spirit of good and the one of evil.

Yes, the wise must speak, not to tell, but to help others find.

The art of keeping silent is the art of hiding the truth without lying.

You should not alert those you are forced to deceive.

Do not argue with anyone. An argument, by overexciting one's self-esteem, produces stubbornness, an enemy of truth and peace.

Never get outraged, nothing deserves our outrage and nothing gives us the right to be outraged. Crimes are disasters and criminals are sick people that we should avoid without feeling hatred towards them.

Hate no man and hold no resentment. Those who hurt us know not what they do, that is, they hand themselves over to a conditioning that makes them worse off than us.

Be gentle and courteous with everyone; but in social relations, never let yourself get absorbed, and withdraw from circles where you would not have some initiative.

To be happy is to devote oneself.

We never complain when we have what we chose.

Never would they have moral pains if they had the power of forgetting.

Let us never miss anyone. We always find again the ones we should always love.

What is Depression if not the dog of that great shepherd that leads men, the vigilant and hungry dog that bites the lazy sheep.

All the suffering of our souls comes from the distraction of our desires and from our stubbornness in carrying out lies.

All the suffering of our hearts comes from wanting to receive and not give, to possess and not improve, to absorb and not immortalize.

The sacred love, the virginal love, the love that is stronger than the tomb, looks only for devotion, and flees frantically before the selfishness of lust.

The great secret of marriage is to postpone the hour of boredom and of waking up [by variety and sublime roleplaying].

Excessive love generates indifference.

The absorbing love is a negative love, while the radiating love is like the sun, its life being to heat up and to illuminate, but it will still shine when it is alone.

To love is to live in those we love, it is to think their thoughts, to anticipate their desires, to share their interests.

Love makes us similar to the thing we love. When you love a cow, you need to be a bull; when you love a bull, you should be a cow.

In the bank of love, the richest is the one who gives.

The faith that moves mountains is nothing more than the coalition of active wills for the fulfillment of a dream or a utopia.

Man can do nothing when alone. Great human strengths are collective strengths.

Two people make a force, three make a group, four make a circle...Two groups make a perfect circle.

A man, if he is a man of genius, is a head without a body. A group unguided by a single infallible authority, is a body without a head.

Twelve men who are active and determined in giving their lives to the spreading of a teacher's idea can change the face of the world: the apostles have proven this well and have performed miracles.

The power of God manifests itself in humanity through two forces: collective faith and indisputable logic.

He who gives, receives, and he who receives, gives; movement is a continual exchange.

Refinement and generosity is the special dream of a woman and it is in this ideal that she finds the stimulus or despair of her love.

Never tell your wife your more secret thoughts — remember the story of Samson and Delilah! As soon as a wife knows her husband through and through she stops loving him...Women always need the unknown and the mysterious, and their love is often nothing more than an insatiable curiosity.

Man only gains possession of such things as honors, wealth, or women, when he does not allow himself under any circumstances to be possessed by them.

Woe to the lover if he changes the magnetic current and pursues that which he should only attract!

A woman always wants others to dare. Her pride decides who she loves; the daring ones are her kings.

Shyness is death, and women, like the earth, accept the law of the strongest.

The more indifferent you are, the easier it will be to make yourself loved.

If you can work, believe, love, and defend yourself; if you are not enslaved by your earthly needs; if your heart can will and your mind understand, then hail, King of Thebes, you are crowned!

Don't be a fool but rather, by your own effort, come to rationally believe that you are something great and strong; the weak and the young will inevitably take you for what you believe yourself to be. It is only a matter of patience and time.

The reason why most people are mediocre is that they are never whole. Honest people sometimes do evil and criminals sometimes do good.

Height is not greatness. In order to be great, let us be useful.

Have the greatest respect for yourself and look at yourself like an unrecognized sovereign who agrees to being in order to reconquer his crown.

The great man is the one who comes seasonably and knows how to innovate opportunely.

You who want to do great things, never tell anyone your most secret thoughts.

Magnetic powers obey two forms of energy: controlled energy and irregular energy.

The alternating use of contrary forces, hot after cold, softness after severity, love after anger, etc., is the secret of continual movement and the prolongation of power.

We simply need to destroy the influence of evil by the power of good.

In this world nothing is accomplished with neediness and haste.

To keep silent is one of the great laws of esotericism. Now, to keep silent is to hide oneself. God is the almighty power that hides itself and Satan is the vain impotence that always tries to show off.

The great magical means of preserving the youth of the body is to prevent the soul from growing old by preciously preserving that original freshness of feelings and thoughts, which the corrupt world calls illusions, and which we will call the primitive mirages of eternal truth.

This profound sentence is one of the great secrets of magic and magnetism: Don't go, it makes one come to you.

There is a balance and there should never be hostility between the man and the woman. The law of union between them is mutual devotion. The woman captivates the man by her charm, and the man empowers the woman by his intelligence. This is the intelligent balance without which we fall into deadly selfishness.

To maintain one's logic in the midst of madmen, one's faith in the midst of superstitions, one's dignity in the midst of buffoons, and one's independence among Panurge's sheep, is of all miracles the rarest, the finest, and the most difficult to accomplish.

A power, invincible if we so wish, was given to us to conquer fate, it is our emotional freedom. With the help of this power, we can correct our destiny and remake our future.

Mystery is the rigorous and indispensable condition of all operations of science.

Women cherish greatness of soul in the same way that men love beauty.

We are the authors of our destinies, and God does not save us without our cooperation.

Nothing equals the electricity of eloquence.

To have the right to own forever, one must will patiently and long.

The will of man is invincible when it is rational and calm. When you walk slowly and always, you definitely end up arriving.

One only really wishes for a thing when one wishes it with all one's heart, to the point of breaking for it one's dearest affections; and with all one's forces, to the point of risking one's health, one's fortune, and one's life.

Strength attracts strength, life attracts life, health attracts health: this is a law of Nature.

Human acts are not only written in the emotional light; their traces are also left upon the face, they modify posture and gait, they change the tone of voice.

When a Christian stops practicing he will not believe for long, but if an unbeliever starts practicing he will eventually believe. Because the will cannot for long be separated from acts.

Don't fear the lion and the lion will fear you. Tell hardship, "I want you to be a pleasure" and it will become a pleasure, even more than a pleasure, a joy.

The law of slow and steady progress is the universal law of nature.

The giver earns more than the recipient. So if you really want to get rich, give.

We never attract effectively the things we lust after, that is, to whose influence we submit.

It is in renouncing the object of lust that we deserve to have the object of true love.

For the wise, to imagine is to see, in the same way that for the magician, to speak is to create.

Man should cultivate all his faculties, develop them, expand his soul, know, love, beautify his life, in a word, make himself happy.

Love one another, that is the law and the prophets! Meditate on and understand this word. And when you have understood it, stop reading, stop seeking, stop doubting, love!

Eliphas Lévi

Man's greatest wisdom
is to choose his
obsession well.

NO METAMORPHOSIS WORKS WITHOUT DESTRUCTION.

t is the imagination alone that accomplishes all miracles.

Learn to will what God desires, and everything you want will definitely happen.